10650254

-Eyed Prince

1

Wataru Mizukami

Translated and adapted by
Jamie Jacobs

Lettered by
North Market Street Graphics

DEL REY
Ballantine Books · New York

Four-Eyed Prince volume 1 is a work of fiction. Names, characters, places, and incidents are the products of the author's imagination or are used fictitiously. Any resemblance to actual events, locales, or persons, living or dead, is entirely coincidental.

A Del Rey Manga/Kodansha Trade Paperback Original

Four-Eyed Prince volume 1 copyright © 2007 by Wataru Mizukami
English translation copyright © 2009 by Wataru Mizukami

All rights reserved.

Published in the United States by Del Rey, an imprint of
The Random House Publishing Group, a division of Random House, Inc., New York.

DEL REY is a registered trademark and the Del Rey colophon is a trademark of Random House, Inc.

Publication rights arranged through Kodansha Ltd.

First published in Japan in 2007 by Kodansha Ltd., Tokyo

ISBN 978-0-345-51624-4

Printed in the United States of America

www.delreymanga.com

2 4 6 8 9 7 5 3 1

Translator/Adapter: Jamie Jacobs
Lettering: North Market Street Graphics

Contents

Honorifics Explained v
Four-Eyed Prince 1
About the Author 172
Translation Notes 173

Honorifics Explained

Throughout the Del Rey Manga books, you will find Japanese honorifics left intact in the translations. For those not familiar with how the Japanese use honorifics and, more important, how they differ from American honorifics, we present this brief overview.

Politeness has always been a critical facet of Japanese culture. Ever since the feudal era, when Japan was a highly stratified society, use of honorifics—which can be defined as polite speech that indicates relationship or status—has played an essential role in the Japanese language. When you address someone in Japanese, an honorific usually takes the form of a suffix attached to one's name (example: "Asuna-san"), is used as a title at the end of one's name, or appears in place of the name itself (example: "Negi-sensei," or simply "Sensei!").

Honorifics can be expressions of respect or endearment. In the context of manga and anime, honorifics give insight into the nature of the relationship between characters. Many English translations leave out these important honorifics and therefore distort the feel of the original Japanese. Because Japanese honorifics contain nuances that English honorifics lack, it is our policy at Del Rey not to translate them. Here, instead, is a guide to some of the honorifics you may encounter in Del Rey Manga.

-san: This is the most common honorific and is equivalent to Mr., Miss, Ms., or Mrs. It is the all-purpose honorific and can be used in any situation where politeness is required.

-sama: This is one level higher than "-san" and is used to confer great respect.

-dono: This comes from the word "tono," which means "lord." It is an even higher level than "-sama" and confers utmost respect.

-kun: This suffix is used at the end of boys' names to express familiarity or endearment. It is also sometimes used by men among friends, or when addressing someone younger or of a lower station.

-chan: This is used to express endearment, mostly toward girls. It is also used for little boys, pets, and even among lovers. It gives a sense of childish cuteness.

Bozu: This is an informal way to refer to a boy, similar to the English terms "kid" and "squirt."

Sempai/ Senpai: This title suggests that the addressee is one's senior in a group or organization. It is most often used in a school setting, where underclassmen refer to their upperclassmen as "sempai." It can also be used in the workplace, such as when a newer employee addresses an employee who has seniority in the company.

Kohai: This is the opposite of "sempai" and is used toward underclassmen in school or newcomers in the workplace. It connotes that the addressee is of a lower station.

Sensei: Literally meaning "one who has come before," this title is used for teachers, doctors, or masters of any profession or art.

-[blank]: This is usually forgotten in these lists, but it is perhaps the most significant difference between Japanese and English. The lack of honorific, known as *yobisute,* means that the speaker has permission to address the person in a very intimate way. Usually, only family, spouses, or very close friends have this kind of permission. It can be gratifying when someone who has earned the intimacy starts to call one by one's name without an honorific. But when that intimacy hasn't been earned, it can be very insulting.

おうじ
Four-Eyed Prince 1

Four-Eyed Prince

∞ Table of Contents

Chapter 1 ——— 004

Chapter 2 ——— 049

Chapter 3 ——— 089

✦ Bonus Story: Mean Boy ——— 129

このインラン女

オレの裏の顔を知ってるからな

バラされていまの平穏を乱されたくな

店でごとはしっていったろ

しゃべったら殺すぞ

お姉さま

フェチかよ

なおすしぐさが…かっこよくて

え

ギッ

ブッ

はぁ？

ブッまいった

こんなバカ妹になるなんて

Let's Start!

Four-Eyed Prince
Chapter 1

Masuda-sempai...
I'm Sachiko Ōhashi, and today my whole life is gonna change.
...I'm in love with you!

I finally decided to go for it and tell him how I feel.
Sorry.
But...
I have no interest in you whatsoever.

What?! Sachi...
...you mean you really told him? The Four-Eyed Prince?!
No way...
...that's basically what happened.
Aaaaand...
1-B
SHATTER
Maybe she saw him rescuing a stray kitten or something sweet like that, and that's why she's fallen so hard for him.
Is that it, Sachi?
No, actually, it's his glasses.
Huh?
He's always dressed all in white, carrying around a bunch of really serious books, and he never talks to anybody. He really does act like a prince!
I dunno. Sounds like he's just stuck-up if you ask me.
Well, everybody's tastes are different. For whatever reason, as far as Sachi is concerned, our sempai is a prince.
Well, yeah!
I don't get it. What do you see in him, anyway?

Oh, it's time for me to leave.
Are you going home early today?
Yeah. I'll see you guys later.
That's one crazy fetish...
He kinda pushes them up like this.
The way he adjusts his glasses...
It's soooooo cool! ♡
But...
Grandma!
Oh, Sachiko!
Today must be the day, huh?
Yeah...
She's really been having a hard time lately, ya know?
I've been kinda playing it off with the two of them and trying to stay positive...
Because I really wanted to have a good day today, no matter what might happen later.

You're late! It's already time to go!!
Sorry! Sorry!
Try to get it together, will ya? Now you've got your new address memorized, right?
Of course!
I'm still opposed to this whole idea, you know.
Huh?
I don't want to let you go back to a mother who abandoned you once before.
This is all happening because I have to be stuck in this stupid wheelchair! You should just come to the nursing home and live with me!
Grandma, don't be silly!
GRAB
YANK
You know there's nothing else we can do. Dad passed away last year...
...and I can't take care of you properly all by myself.

Anyway, something really, **really** lousy happened to me today!
I should be in the depths of despair right now!
What? What happened?!
But actually, it's really OK...
VROOOOOOM
I'll come and visit you every week!
That's right.
...because it just means there's no way things could possibly get any worse today.
So don't worry about me, I'll be just fine!
I loved Sempai for so long.
Sachiko...

Wow... this place is pretty nice, isn't it?
Mom must be making a lot of money these days.
But I do feel sa or lone thinkin about right no
Right! Hang in there, Sachiko!!
I guess that's because I've got nothing to lose anymore.
And that just means there's nothing for me to be afraid of!
My mom left 15 years ago and I've never met her, not even once.
To be honest, I'm kinda scared of meeting her. I barely know anything about her.
Kotato Ryōko
Kanagawa-kun,
Kawasaki-shi
XX-ku, OO-chō
8-4-5
Apt. #405
This is it...
ピンポーン
DING-DONG
Here goes...
Although I did hear she's got another kid besides me.
Well, I'll just do my best to try to make friends with them.

Yes?
CREEEEEAK
S-sorry! I must have the wrong apartment.
TURN
Wait a minute. This *is* the right apartment... isn't it?
Kozato Ryōko
405
Great, now I'm seeing things. Must be the aftereffects of being rejected!
I guess I *did* have the right apartment after all...

But what the heck are *you* doing here, Sempai?!
Huh?
There you are! Oh, Sachi-chan, I've been waiting for you!!
Uh...
...Mom?
That's right—it's me! Eeeeek! It's been so long!! You've gotten so big!
But the last time I saw you, you were just a baby—so of course you've grown since then! Hahahahaha!!!
Wh... who's this?
Oh! Let me introduce you.
Oh, good. At least she's... energetic...
Um, Mom?

This is Akihiko Masuda. He's 17, which would make him your big brother!
Akihiko...
This is your cute little sister, Sachiko Ōhashi. Starting today, we'll all be living together as one big happy family! ♡
Urg...
So even though I introduced you as siblings, you're actually not related by blood at all. ♡
But Mom, your maiden name is "Kozato," right? So your last name and his last name are...
You gotta be kidding me!!!
Oh, Akihiko is my ex-husband's son.

Oh no, is that the time already?!
I've got to work late tonight, so...
Akihiko, help Sachi-chan get settled in, OK?
SILENCE
Um... But...
OK.
Got it.
POINT
And this is my room. But I'm studying right now, so don't bother me.
POINT
That's the bathroom, and that's the kitchen.
What the heck am I supposed to do now??
This is your room.
Huh? Oh— OK!
Your stuff's already in there.
Huh?
As usual, your mom hasn't really considered anybody's point of view but her own.

What the heck? I really thought things couldn't get any worse!
SLAM
パタン
O... opposed??
So mean...!
And now I find out the guy who broke my heart this morning is my new stepbrother...?
What I'm trying to say is... I'm opposed to the idea of us living together.

Aaaagh! How the heck am I supposed to live under the same roof with him?!
But now we're siblings! *Siblings*!!
When I saw his face at the door, my heart just stopped.
TWITCH
...Live under the same roof...
Even though he totally turned me down, I still like him.
My beloved Sempai...
I'll get to see him like this... And like this...
SPLURT

TOTALLY FANTASIZING
And in the living room...
...We might be like that!
In the bathroom...
EEEEEK!!
...It might be like this!
...we can whisper sweet nothings in each others' ears! ♡
And outside on the veranda, where my mom won't think to look for us...
Wait a minute!
O'oh!
Why am I sitting around here daydreaming? He said he was opposed to the two of us living together.
Where's he going at this hour...?
Sempai?!
—Hey!
ばっ
LEAP

Don't tell me he decided to run away from home!
It was bad enough to be rejected... but living with somebody who can't stand being in the same house with you would be even worse!!
KA-BOOOOOOM
—I've got to convince him to change his mind.
Better go after him!
TURN
So I did.
I rushed down here trying to find him...
Kabuki-chô Ichibangai
...but where the heck am I?!
Watch where you're going!!
HEEEEEEE...
Whoa!
SHOVE
Wh... what the...?

...Sigh...
ザザー
DOWNPOUR
No way...
Oh no! I lost sight of him...
SPLAT
Hey, Master, it's raining really hard out here.
It's probably just a passing shower, though.
カラーン
CREEEEAK
What am I doing here, anyway?
I should just go home...

Oh...
Sorry to startle you!
I was just trying to get out of the rain—
You're soaking wet! You'll catch a cold for sure!
Quick, come inside!
Huh?
SHOVE
Wait! Master...
SHOVE
Akira-chan, bring her a towel and some dry clothes!
Oh my...
!
Oh my goodness! Are you all right?!

...so why don't you wait inside until they're done? ♡
I'll put your clothes in the dryer...
O—OK.
You've got pretty strange taste, ya know.
Wow! You look great! ♡
EEEEEEEEK!!!
I've never been in a place like this before!
よろ～
WOBBLE
Uh... um...
Wow—

You're new around here, but you're not even polite enough to say hello to us! And cozying up to Akira on top of that? You've got a lot of nerve!
Huh? Who's Akira??
And what exactly is your business with Akira?
What do you say, girls? Shall we teach her some manners?
N-no way!!
I've told you all before... no making any scenes in the bar.
OK, ladies?

あぜん
DUMBSTRUCK
This kind of place tends to attract girls like that.
Oh, Akira! We're sorry!!
Squee!! It's Akira!
Here. Drink this before you go.
Oh...
STEAM
Oh! It's the Akira-chan Special: hot milk with a shot of brandy!
Th... thank you.

...My dad passed away a year ago.
Well...
What?
TEA
Lightly Sweetened
NUDGE.
The day he died was a rainy day, just like today.
...but it would have made me feel worse if everybody else felt sorry for me. So I tried to be strong.
It was really sad...
I'm OK! Really!
Sachi...

But then today, that very same guy rejected me and broke my heart.
...Oh yeah?
What about the guy? Are you still interested in him?
くね SQUIRM
Waaaah! What a moving story!!
くね SQUIRM
Hmmm...
GLUG
Here.
...this guy appeared out of nowhere and handed me a warm drink, just like this one.
Right at that moment, even though I'd never met him or talked to him before...
And ever since then, I've always thought of him as my prince.

Hey...
That's right! Who cares if he broke my heart?!
SLAM
Not... one... bit! I'm totally over him!
GRAB
Don't make a scene out here.
Huh...?
If you're looking for a way to de-stress...
...I've got the perfect thing!
Wow!
WHAP
Mizukami

Here, you give it a try.
O-OK...
But...
...I don't know if I can do it!!
What's he doing? Did he just put his hand on my waist?!
This guy looks like a nice guy on the outside, but underneath it all, this is what he's really like—a "gentleman of the night"! Scary!!
Hey...
...Stay focused.
Agh!!
TWITCH

FLASH
FLASH!
THWOK
Oh...
I did it!!
はっ
GASP
S-sorry!
Didn't mean to get so... close...
ぱっ
LEAP
GRAB
いっ
Huh?

It's OK.
Why don't I make you forget all about that other guy?
"Forget"?

Make me forget...
...about my Sempai?
No...!
SHOVE
What do you think you're doing?!

Huh??
ZZZZZZZ
What the...?!
WHUMP
A-ki-ra-chan...
My goodness!
Don't tell me you knocked her out with that hot milk and brandy...!
Psh!
Who gets drunk after one little drink like that?!
Oh dear...
SQUEEZE

Mmmm... feels so soft...
Jeez!
What else was I supposed to do? It's not like I could just leave you at the bar!
Hey hey hey... why so cranky?
Get down already, you big lush!
Whaaa...?
しぽ
ちっ
BLINK
Hey, everybody! This guy right here...
He might *look* all sweet and innocent, but the truth is... he can't keep his hands to himself!!
ケラケラ
CACKLE CACKLE
Cut it out!
Hey!!
Saaaaay...
...how come you're carrying me, Akira-san?

Wow!
It's so pretty!
It's amazing. I didn't know there was such a nice view here.
Uh...
Hey—

YOU BIG JERK!!!
STUNNED
ぎょっ
Akihiko Masuda, I oughta kick your butt!!!
Just leave me alone! After the day I've just had, I need to shout a little or else I'm gonna explode!!
What the heck are you...

With one sentence, you wiped out all the courage I managed to scrape together just to talk to you!
Who do you think you are?! I had a crush on you for over a year, even though everybody else said you had a bad attitude!
And now on top of all that, we're going to be *siblings*?! WHAT THE HECK?!?!?!
はぁ
HUFF
HUFF
はぁ
...So are you done now? I hope?
But the worst part is...

And that makes *me* the biggest jerk of all!!
The worst part is that I still like you! Even after everything you've put me through, you jerk!

Hahaha! Well! I feel *much* better now!!
You...
Heh heh...
DRIP
Ooooh...
Ooooooooooh...
WAAAAAAAH!!
AAAAAAH!!
Goodbye...
Goodbye, my first love.

I'll be strong. I promise.
As of tomorrow, you and I will be strictly siblings to each other from here on out.
SNIFF
SNIFF
SNIFF
So tonight...
...just let me cry it out, OK?
HIC

Huh?
...What are you still doing here?
...Did you just pass out again?
ZZZZZ
What's that supposed to mean?
Would you really expect me to just leave you here and go on my merry...
こっん
FLOP

Goodbye...
Jeez...
Sempai...

Good morning.
BLINK
ぱちっ
Huh...?
Oh. Good morni...
JOLT
がばっ

What happened?!
What the— My clothes!!
Looks like you're feeling better. You're probably not even hung over, are you?
Um... uh... I...
Anyway...
Doesn't it bother you, being kinda... well... *easy*??
Huh...?
I felt a little sorry for you last night, but...
now, seeing you in such a compromising position...

A-Akira-san...
W-what the heck did I do?!
At school I wear these to keep girls from noticing me.
RUMPLE
RUMPLE
GRAB
But I guess it doesn't really matter in the end. Whether it's you or some other girl...
...in the end, you're all just sluts.
Se-

Sempai?!?!?!
Wha–
Wha–
Wha–
My Four-Eyed Prince... and the bartender from last night... are both the same guy?!
I...
The Akira/ Bartender personality is more like the real me.
Although "Akira" is a fake name, of course.
I can't believe you tricked me!!
I didn't trick you. If you had half a brain you would have realized it was me a long time ago.

You... You're so mean...!
—Wait a minute.
Sigh... I can't believe I'm gonna be stuck with an idiot like you for a younger sister.
Now I'm *really* starting to feel sorry for myself.
So if you really think of me as a younger sister, then why did you bring me home and take advantage of me?!
ばっ
LEAP
FREEZE
You just called me...
your younger sister...
Does this mean he's accepted the fact that I'm going to be living here?

Oh...!
ドキッ
BA-BUMP
ニヤッ
GRIN
Looks like you're still way too immature for that!
Who would "take advantage" of a kid like you?

EEEE EEEEK
I'm Sachiko Ōhashi, age 16.
!!
And one thing's for sure:
...my life just took a 180° turn.
As of yesterday...
Ryōko Kozato–Akihiko Masuda–Sachiko Ōhashi

Four-Eyed Prince
Chapter 2

Sachi.
Yes?
As of today, I've officially become your older brother.
Huh?
But the way I feel about you isn't the way a brother ought to feel about a sister.
I love you, Sachi.
Really?

YANK
ROLL
CRASH
Aaaagh!
WAKE UP!
SQUEEE
Me too...
Mmm... mmph...
Hi, everybody.
It's been about a week since my name officially changed from "Sachiko Ōhashi" to "Sachiko Kozato."
Oh... I guess that was just a dream.
What was just a dream?
Nothing!
I made breakfast, so hurry up and eat before it gets cold!

Let me help you put it all out on the table. ♡
No, wait! Don't ...!
GRAB
SLIP
Yum! Maybe this whole sibling relationship thing is gonna be smoother sailing than I thought!
Wow!
Another delicious breakfast! Sempai, you're a culinary genius!
What... is... wrong... with... you?!
How on earth a klutz like you made it for so long with just your grandmother to save you from yourself is beyond me.
His words are usually harsh...
...but underneath it all, my Four-Eyed Prince really is kind to me.

I was really surprised when I realized that he and my Four-Eyed Prince were the same person.
Then right after that, I met "Akira the Bartender."
It's hard to believe that just one week ago, I was feeling totally crushed because he had rejected me.
I have no interest in you whatsoever.
ズガーン
SHOCK
Now we're living together as brother and sister...
...which means we're around each other all the time, so my chances of getting together with him just got a whole lot better!
Hey, wait up!
I'll come with you!
ちゃ...
CREAK...
No thanks.
I'm OK with the fact that we're brother and sister now...
...but like I said, I don't want the whole world to know about it.

Especially because you know about my double life now.
The last thing I want is for a bunch of rumors to get started about that. I like my peace and privacy.
So rest assured... if you tell anybody, I'll kill you.
Whaaaaat?!
With who? Your new brother?!
Huh?!
N-no! I wasn't talking about him...
GULP
Aw, come on! What are you trying to hide? You haven't told me anything about him at all, Sachi!
Well, so much for the idea of getting closer to him!
It'd be nice if we could at least be just a little friendly with each other...

"Coolest in School Contest"?
Calling all good-looking guys!
High School's First Annual Coolest in School Contest
Winner receives an all-expenses-paid hot springs vacation!
So!
If you're looking for a way to get to know your brother better, why not try this?
The sponsors and contestants both dress in costumes and compete as a pair.
That's right! Girls find guys they want to sponsor as their partners, and anybody can enter the contest.
殺
KILL YOU
CRUMPLE
Hmm... this could be fun...
Sachi, you said your new brother is a pretty good-looking guy, right?
I'm on the organizing committee and we need to recruit some more contestants.

We're still just getting used to each other as siblings, so I don't think he'll want to do it... But on the other hand, this could be my big chance!
KILL YOU
SQUEEZE
KILL
HOT SPRING
Ow...
oooh...
KILL YOU
ouch...
SQUEEZE
A hot spring...?
If you win, you get a free trip to a hot spring!
But why not??
No... I don't think he would go for it.
That's it! Of course!!
My Four-Eyed Prince told me not to be too friendly with him at school or else he would kill me.
But he didn't say anything about getting friendly with Akira!!
BA-BUMP
BA-BUMP
BA-BUMP
BA-BUMP
?
EH-HEH
GASP
Huh?
I got it! I'll ask Akira!!

Ta-da! It's an entry form for the Coolest in School Contest!
Entry Form
NO. 3
Sponsor:
Sachiko Kozato
Contestant:
Akira Kozato
What's that?
What do you mean "ta-da"?!
You idiot!!
What do you think you're doing, entering me in a contest like that?! I told you I didn't want people to find out about us at school, remember?
And how come you put Akira's name on that form?!
You didn't say anything about keeping Akira a secret!
You just don't seem to get it, do you?

Uh-oh, I'm losing him! Gotta figure out how to talk him into this...
What's wrong with entering as Akira?
You'd be a huge hit with the girls!
STEAM
Cause if we win...
Wh-what do you mean, I'm dumb?!
—Jeez. I knew you were dumb, but I didn't think you were *this* dumb!!
Right! So that's why you should enter!
Present-ing... Akira! We love Akira! Goooooo Akira!!
Ooooh! He might see me naked! ♡
I'm a little embar-rassed...
Wouldn't that be *amazing*?!
SQUEAL
I'll have to take my glasses off. I can't see your beautiful naked body with them all fogged up like this.

Really? You will?!
...Come on! Is he going to say yes or not?!
とぼけい PLEASE!
—I see.
OK. I'll do it.
What do you think of this?
Something like that.
GASP
But how come?
Are you some kind of huge hot springs fan or something?
I don't know why he said yes, but I guess it doesn't matter!
So it's a costume contest, right?
What should we dress up as?
Oh! I've been thinking about that, and I came up with an idea.
?.?
He's really going to do it??

What's the big deal? You're going to change clothes too, right?
Oh! I-I'm sorry!!
FWISH
ばっ

Ee-eee-eek!!!!
SLAM
Let me help you get dressed!
H-hold on a second.
What does he think he's doing??

Hey, Sachi, welcome back! Sorry about that, it was just a little costume-related joke.
Sa-sa-sa-sa... "Sachi" ?!?!?
Ever since then...
...things have been going pretty well between the two of us.
Now that I've discovered his other personality,
whether he's in Akira mode or Four-Eyed Prince mode...
Move a little closer to me.
O-OK!
...he's been a whole lot nicer to me.
That costume looks cute on you.
C-cute?!
Apparently he bought a few other things besides costume supplies...

FLIP
Oh...
...that must be my phone.
RRRRR
I think the "Akira" side of Sempai likes to show off to me a little.
But that's OK.
CREAK
I don't mind...
Your mom's working late again,
so she said for us to go ahead and take our baths and then go to sleep.
I just hope we win.

Looks like you're sleeping already, though.
ZZZZZZ
Hey, wake up.
You'll catch a cold sleeping out here.
SHAKE
Nyuh? I *am* awake...
No you're not!
Come on.
Huh...?
Sigh...

Sempai, you have such a nice smile.
EH-HEH
!
People who say silly things like that should go to sleep and never wake back up.
Eh he he...
I really like your smile, *Akira-san*.

Hey, Akira-chan.
Huh?
I really appreciate the polishing job...
キュッ
RUB
RUB
キュッ
...but do you think you could do that to the bar glasses instead of my face?
...Sorry about that.
That's OK, but...
It's not like you to be so preoccupied.
Anyway, isn't today supposed to be your last big practice day before the contest?
!!
zzz...
すっ
……

Hmmm...
Well, I only agreed to it on a whim in the first place.
And that girl was just getting way too annoying. I didn't feel like hanging out with her anymore.
Yeah.
But I'm not doing the contest anymore.
Oh?
That's too bad. And here I thought the two of you were getting to be really close.
Huh?

The real you...
...is neither Akira nor the boy with the glasses.
But you're afraid to let her see who you really are, so now you're just running away.
Wha...
カランッ
SLAM
Hey!
There you are!
How come you skipped out on our practice? Well, whatever—we've still got a little time left. Come on, let's go!
YANK
ばっ!
Whoa!

I'm not going to be in the contest.
What?? Why is he doing this?!
I know he was just kinda going along with it when he said yes at first, but...
What?! Why not?
No reason, really.
It's just too much of a pain in the butt.

Sigh...
Ever since you came on the scene, my life has totally sucked. Now my pay's even gonna get docked because I had to come back here and straighten things out with you.
Look, don't make a scene out here in the bar, OK? Let's go in the back.
Why are you just changing your mind all of a sudden?!
I really thought we were getting closer to each other...
Whose fault do you think all that is? I'll tell you—it's *yours*!
Do you think maybe you could stop ruining my life for five minutes?
That's *my* line.

For someone who doesn't know a thing about me, you sure do have a lot of opinions, huh?
Who do you think you are, running around pretending to be two completely different people? What's up with that anyway?!
Oh, so that's your problem, huh?
I thought you were into the guy with the glasses. Now all of a sudden you've got the hots for "Akira."
That's not—

The fact that I'm living with your mom, even though I'm not really her son or related to her by blood at all...
You've never even wondered about that, have you?
...Huh?
SMACK
My real dad got himself into a bunch of debt and then took off.
In the end, when I finally had nowhere else to go, the person who wound up taking me in was Ryōko-san.
That was when he was still with Ryōko-san and the three of us were all living together.
She was working like crazy to earn enough money to pay back my father's debts.
I had to put on two different faces in order to fit in and be liked.
Our family was splitting up, so I got bounced around between a bunch of different relatives for a while.

So that's my story. Did you know all that about me?
But in the end, I'm still not her real son or anything, so I want to hurry up and become independent as soon as possible. That's why I decided to take advantage of my stunning good looks and get a job working here.
They're just masks.
What you think you see is nothing but a façade.
GRAB
...That's not true.
You've seen both sides of my personality now, so you just figured you knew everything there was to know, didn't you?
But neither one of those guys is the *real* me.

Sigh...
Sempai, you have such a nice smile.
The contest is tomorrow!
I'll see you there!!
What?
What I'm seeing isn't some fake version of you.
I know it's not.
That time you smiled at me... *that* was the real you! Am I right?

Contest Waiting Room 10:00
The day of the contest:
CHATTER
CHATTER
SLAM
I'll see you there...
Aki...
Really? He's here?!
HUH?
Sachi!
Where's this infamous big brother of yours? You two are on next!!
He might not be coming.
What?!
But... but...
Oh no!
Kozato-san, your partner's here!
Executive Committee

Well, the competition is definitely getting intense!
Who will be named the winner of our Coolest in School Contest?!
COOLEST IN SCHOOL
AHHH
OOOH
And now for our next contestant:
...Sachiko Kozato-san!
STEP
Her partner's a strong and silent type who works by night.
Ladies and gentlemen, I give you the high school student/bartender, Akira!!
SQUEEE!
Akira?! I've heard of him!!
Huh? Akira? Who's that?
DUN

What the heck is supposed to be "cool" about him??
That's not Akira!
Isn't that supposed to be Sachi's brother...?
What?? The Four-Eyed Prince?!
STARE
This thing is heavy...
Why did you decide to come after all?

Well...
...it seemed to be pretty important to you.
But how come you're wearing your glasses?
Everybody's gonna know that you and I are siblings now, Sempai.
It's OK.
I'm used to wearing my glasses when I'm at school anyway.
Sempai...
M-moving right along...
According to the entry form, these two are dressed as a dashing young pirate and his kidnapped princess!

Well, everybody has different tastes... ahem...
Anyway, it seems that you two recently became siblings by marriage. Is that correct?
Um, yes.
"Four-Eyed Prince"?
Heh!
What makes *him* a prince??
CACKLE SNICKER
He looks totally lame!!
That girl must have some kind of glasses fetish or something!
HA HA
LAUGHTER
SCRIPT
I-it appears that our pirate also goes by the nickname "Four-Eyed Prince."
GRAB
Everybody, please—!
Huh?

SILENCE
You're all a bunch of idiots!
It's pretty stupid to think you know somebody just from what you see on the surface.
I used to be like that too, embarrassing as it is to admit it.

But anyway...
I like this guy.
Anybody got
a problem with
that?

Who cares about your "real" self, anyway?
You...
Your Four-Eyed Prince identity and your Akira identity are both a part of you, Sempai.
And I like *all* of who you are.

SLIDE
カチャ…
Wha...
CHATTER
ザワ
...You really are too much sometimes, you know that?
CHATTER
ザワ
STARE
じっ
SWOOP
Huh?!
Sempai...

I don't think I'll be needing those glasses anymore.
WHAAAAAT?!
えぇぇ!?
Wow! That guy is amazing!!
It is Akira!!
That guy with the glasses— he's Akira!!
O-oh my!
We have a winner!!

PRIZE
Thanks. We appreciate it.
わあああああ
SQUEEEEEAL
はあ
HUFF
はあ
HUFF
Phew...

Well, now that everybody knows who you really are, I don't know what's going to happen at school tomorrow.
That's OK.
You're so heavy!!!
Well excuuuuuuse me!!
I didn't ask you to carry me off like that!!
はー
せー
WHEEZE
PUFF
BA-BUMP
It doesn't matter to me anymore.

So anyway, about that hot springs trip...
Uh...
Who do you want to go with? The guy with the glasses? Or Akira?
GRIN
Um...
Ha ha ha!
I was kidding, you know...
B-both!!!

Four-Eyed Prince

Chapter 3

Wow!
PRIZE
Hi there!
I'm Sachiko Kozato, the girl who'll be going on a hot springs vacation with my sempai tomorrow!
SPECIAL REPORT
Natural Hot Springs With an Amazing View
Limestone Caves Nearby!!
Hey, Mom, look at this!
The hot spring we're going to got written up in this magazine!
Wow, it looks amazing!
I wish I were going with you!
Hey, Sempai, check this ou—
Hehe! Well, you can come next time!
YAAAAAWN

Hey! Do you want to go on this trip or not?!
And how come you came home so late last night?
You'd better not have forgotten to pack or something...!
Huh?
I had to work till after midnight, that's why I got back so late.
I can't believe you!!
Huh? The trip? Is that tomorrow?
Let's see... gotta wash my hair and put on my school clothes...
Because of his family circumstances growing up, Sempai had two identities that he put on for the outside world: the "serious guy with glasses" and "Akira the bartender."
But when he's around me, he doesn't need to wear those masks anymore.
Or at least, that's what I thought...!
But maybe he hasn't really changed after all.
がっしり
CLENCH

CH-CHN'
Phew! Thank goodness we made it!!
CH-CHN'
I had big plans for this trip...
...but I'm starting to have a bad feeling about this whole thing.
BEEEEEEEEP
OK, OK... I already said I was sorry.
Let's go find our seats.
We almost missed the train because *you* overslept, Sempai!
TUG
Here, give me your bag.
!!
He's so mean!
Aaaagh!
Wait! Wait!!
Take the window seat.

SHOVE
N...
No, that's all right! You go ahead!
You think I'm gonna let you off easy just because you're acting like it's no big deal?!
Not so fast!
SURPRISE
What?!
OK, OK! Stop pushing me!
SHOVE
Mmm... I'm sleepy.
I don't want anybody looking at him but me! He's all mine!!
SWOOOOON
He's so gorgeous with those glasses!

Huh. There's another couple sitting across from us.
Here, Yuriko, put your jacket on.
I don't want you to catch cold. OK?
Hmph.
Wow...
Crap, he's already asleep!!
zzzzzz
What a nice thing to do!
OK, I'll do the same.
Sempai!

GLANCE
I said I'm *fine*, Kenta. Stop bugging me!
BA-BUMP
PEEK
Uh-oh. Sounds like a fight.
Whoops...
EH-HEH...
Ha ha...
Are you two taking a trip together, too?
So we're both going to the same place? And staying at the same inn? No way! What a coincidence!
The two of us have been going out for a while. I guess after two people have been together for so long, the relationship kinda cools down a bit, ya know?
SNORE
Sheesh, we're not even *dating* and our relationship has already cooled down...
How about if we make some plans together?
Huh?

Jeez, you guys are loud!
RRRRGH...
Ahahaha!!
Sempai, go back to sleep!
Hey, we could even exchange partners! Whaddaya say?
Whaaaaaaat?!
Wow... hey, wait a second...
Kenta, what's wrong with you?
How could you say something so rude and self-entered?!
I was just kidding!

That girl's boyfriend is totally hot!!
Huh?
Let's trade!!
If I get to be with this guy, then I'm all for it!
Yuriko ... !!
FREEZE
STOP!!!
What on earth is wrong with you people?! There's *no way* I'm switching partners!!
WIPE WIPE

ote: This is a antasy, so her ashion sense is out 120% better than normal.
BA-BUMP!!
First I'm gonna knock his socks off with a sexy bikini pose on the beach!
This trip is really important to the two of us!!
Sachi's "Rose-Colored Glasses" Plan
Then we'll move on to a carefully contrived "accidental" kiss in the limestone caverns!
And then the two of us will...
CENSORED

...You were actually *planning* all of that??
UM...
Microphone Connected Directly to Brain
Whoops! I can't believe I just said that out loud!!
I can't believe this.
Sigh...
Great. My little sister, plotting some kind of crazy assault on me.
What? She's your little sister? That means you're not a couple, so what's the problem?
Uh... well...
Right, Kenta?
S-sure!
No problem!
H-hey!!
Right??
GLARE

It's all settled, then!
You'll leave your glasses off while you're with me, won't you?
Here, let me style your hair too while I'm at it.
Oh!
It'll really look good when I get done with it.
N-no! Sempai!!
You're supposed to be on vacation with me!
Say no to her! Please!!
...
Kenta, hand me your hair gel!
不穏な空気
UNEASY ATMOSPHERE
SHOCK
No waaaaaaaay!!!
Sure. Why not.
SHOCK
ガーン!!

I'm gonna go get changed.
Wow!
The ocean is gorgeous!
SPLASH
Hey, Sempai!
WHISPER
WHISPER
Oh, I don't need my glasses.
If I come back with a tan line around my eyes, the Master'll kill me.
GRIN
Besides, leaving them off might be more fun, considering the circumstances.
Let's put your glasses back on, OK?
It's still too early in the day for you to be getting into your Akira role.
Huh?
And hey, by the way, I thought you said you didn't like that type of fashionista girl!
Hey!
Eeee!
He's so cute!
Squee!!
Oooh!

Feast your eyes on this totally tantalizing swimsuit, Sempai! This should *definitely* get his attention—
I... I'm going to go get changed, too!
Grrr! They're all checking him out!!
SNAG
I...I don't believe this.
KAAAAW
SNICKER
SNICKER
Come back here, you stupid bird!
H-Hey!
KAAAAW
KAAAAW
SPLAT
Poop

Hey, what are you guys doing?
What do you think, Akira-kun?
Does this suit look good on me?
Wow... she looks incredible...
THUNK
It's a good thing Sachi lost her suit.
Compared to you, she probably would have looked like a three-year-old trying to fill out a bikini.
GAGA
Oh yeah. You have great taste.
Why thank you! ♡

He... he's so *mean*!
STARE
ポー
Don't just stand there gawking at her swimsuit! Do something!!
TICKED OFF
むきー
Uh...
You *are* her boyfriend, aren't you?!
Whatever. I don't care.
Not about some girl who'll flirt with any guy she sees.
What did you just say?!
Never mind.
Let's get outta here and go do something else. She doesn't have a bathing suit to wear anyway.
GLARE
FROZEN
Let's check out the caves.
Limestone Caves
300 Meters Ahead
R-right! That's a good idea!
Maybe we should just go our separate ways from here and...
OK.

Wh...
But let's stick with the partners we have now, OK? ♡
Whyyyyyyy?!?!
Wow! This is beautiful!

イライライライライ
ANGER
ANGER
ANGER
ANGER
Let's go over there!
Look, there's some kind of un-identified species in here!
Oh yeah! Real cute, isn't it?!
ずかずかずか
STOMP STOMP STOMP
I can't believe he's putting the moves on another girl like that!!
What do the two of them think they're doing?!
Caution- Slippery Ground
Watch out—it's slippery over there!
What?!
Uh-oh...
SLIP
すべるっ

GRAB
Hey... be careful.
Hey...
I didn't realize it was so slippery! Thank you! ♡
Oh my good-ness!
Are you OK?
.....

Would you help me up?
Oh! Sure. Here, take my hand...
SLIP
BONK
BONK
WHUMP
!!!
くす
SNICKER
くす
SNICKER
Jeez, what's wrong with you?!
Sorry about that!
Kenta, you jerk.

Listen, you...
Hey.
Why do you look like you're having such a good time?
How about you and I becoming a couple for *real*?

Oh no!
Ow...
STEP
I... I'm so sorry!!
SHOVE
That's it!! Now you're really crossing the line!!
Eeek!
SMACK

But so far, coming here with you has been nothing but EXHAUSTING.
SHOCK
Wha...
Do you know why people go on these hot springs trips?
They do it to relax.

GUST
Like two puppies left out in the cold
What?
ICY STARE
Uh...
Nothing...
Are you OK? Can you walk?
Yeah. There's a first-aid kit in my room... would you walk me there?
I-in your room?! Hey! Yuriko...
Sigh...
If everything had gone according to plan...
ぴちゃ…ん
DRIP

...the two of us would be enjoying this amazing view *together*.
What am I even doing here?
Sempai?!
Is that...?
SPLASH
カシャッ
Hey, Sachi-chan.
Well, let him do whatever he wants. I don't care any—

Well, this is the co-ed bathing area, isn't it?
The water feels great!
Kenta-san, what are you doing here?!
W-wait a minute!
B-but...
...where's Yuriko-san?
ANNOYED
Oh...
I don't know and I don't care.

She's hanging all over another guy right in front of me! Why should I care about a girl like that?!
COVER UP
Well, it was *your* idea to switch partners in the first place!
...then why don't the two of us have some fun, too?
NO!!!
ズキ
TWITCH
Hey, it's not like your boyfriend cares about you, either.
So if they're both going to be like that...

Hold it right there.
Sempai...!

I don't believe it!
FWAP
You came to rescue me—
Mmph!
Huh?
Yuriko-san's here, too?
RUMPLE
You've really got some guts, don't you?
Bringing your girlfriend to a hot springs resort and then bathing with another girl.
N-no! That's not...
Oh, don't get me wrong—I don't mind. In fact...
Huh?!
Since you seem to be OK with that kind of thing, I might just do the same myself.

N-no way!
Stop it!
Don't!!
...Y-you...

ばっ!!
GRAB
You JERK!!!
Get your hands off my Yuriko!!
Hmph.
PUNCH
ズドン
GLUG
You spineless jerk!
And you, Yuriko! You're supposed to be my girl! Don't you have any conscience at all?!
SPLASH
SPLASH ゴボッ ゴボッ
ばっしゃーんっ
GAAAH!
SPLASH

Yuriko...?
Kenta... this is the first time you've ever really stood up for me.
...Huh?
Sempai...!
しらーん
PLAYING DUMB
ふり
So I got Akira-kun to pretend to come on to me.
Can I ask you for a favor?
Kenta, you're always so kind and gentle with me that sometimes I find myself taking advantage of you and not appreciating you as much as I should.
And I really don't like that about myself.

I'm sorry... for testing your love for me like that...
No, I'm the one who should apologize.
I'm the one who made you feel so desperate that you had to come up with a plan like this in order to feel appreciated.
I'm sorry I didn't realize how you felt.
I love you, Yuriko.
Oh, Kenta...!
AHEM
Well, I think it's kinda nice.
...the two of us getting caught up in somebody else's domestic dispute??
So basically what this all boils down to is...
WHAT?!
This is his idea of "nice"??
I mean, when you consider the lengths that girl went to...
it must mean that she really cares about him, right?

That's the kind of argument that two people can only have if they share a really long history together, you know?
Huh. I never thought about it like that...
We are just starting out, after all.
For now...
But Sempai, I can't believe what a good act you put on.
You had me completely fooled!
I guess I was trying to rush things a little bit with him and me.
Well, when it comes to acting, I've had a lot of experience.
ADJUST

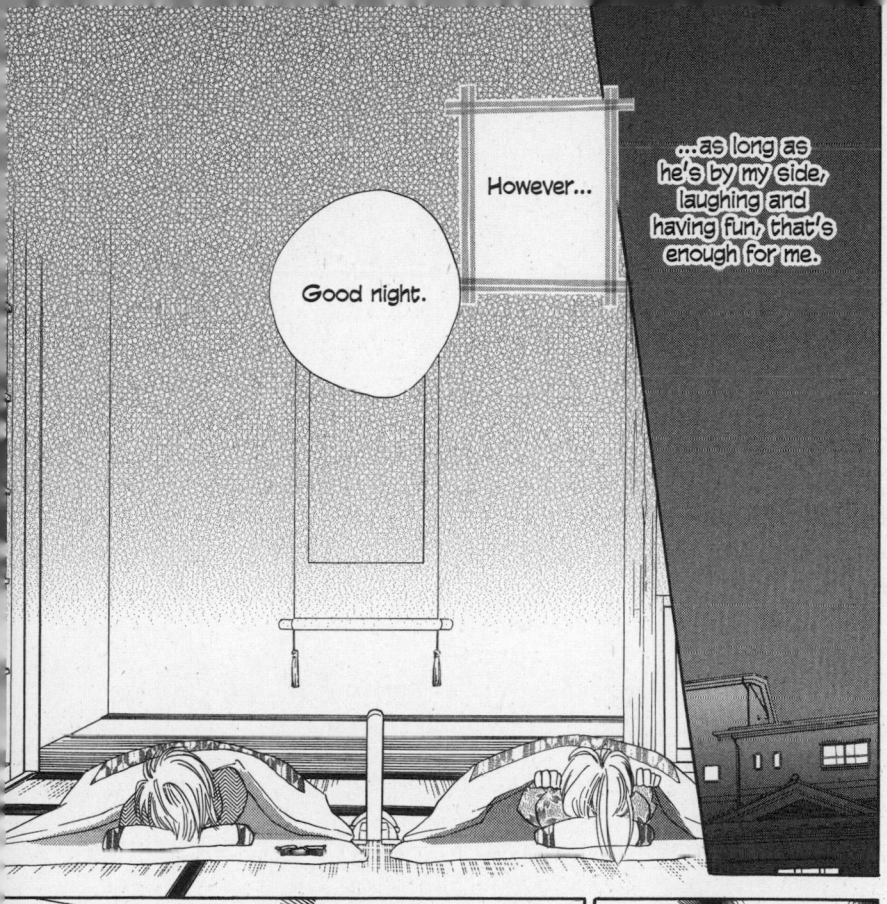
...as long as he's by my side, laughing and having fun, that's enough for me.
However...
Good night.

I'll just take a little bitty peek at him while he's sleeping...
Is it too much to ask for him to get the tiniest bit excited over me? Sheesh!
You know, I'm a healthy young teenage girl.
SNEAK...
コソ…

Doesn't he think these sleeping arrangements are a little bit much?!
SNOOOOORE
くかーっ
And he fell asleep so quickly, too!

くり
GRAB
W-whoops!
...What are you doing?
Go to sleep.
ぴきーん
FREEZE
SIT UP!
いっ
Hey!
Mmmmm...?
ぱっ
BLINK
ちっ
No way.
A-are we getting ready to take it to the next level...?!

Jeez, you're already asleep again?!
SHOVE
ROLL-OVER
SNOOOOORE
What the heck is wrong with him?
What does he think I am, a teddy bear or something?!
But... he looks so cute...
OK... fine.

ぎゅっ
SQUEEZE
I guess we've got to take it one step at a time...

...if the two of us are gonna keep getting closer...
ぱっ
BLINK
ちら
SNOOZE
すかー
...I can't sleep.

Today's our last day here, so let's really make it count! We'll make up for having such a lousy day yesterday!
SHIIIIINE
ぴーかんっ
OK!
Right!!
So... did the two of them wind up living happily ever after?
Hey! You two are *not* invited!!
Hey...
How come you look so tired?
To Be Continued in Volume 2

Mean Boy
Karuizawa:
ピンポン
DING DONG
Hello?!
My name is Sakamoto— I'm the new housekeeper!
Aren't you a little late?
ガチャ
CREEEEAK
Wow, what a beautiful house...!
Oh!!

Mean Boy

I'm a freshman in high school, and this summer vacation I agreed to take over my older cousin's summer job.
But imagine my surprise...
Cousin: Satsuki
Thanks for helping me out!
I really appreciate it, Kōme!
What are *you* doing here, Sakamoto-san?
W-well, there was kind of a last-minute emergency, and...
Aw, man...
I was expecting some hot young college student or something.
You're not the one who sent in this resume.
Well, the last name's the same, but...
...when I found out I'd be cleaning house for *Aoi Izumi*!!
STARE
STARE
You've really got a lot of nerve! How rude!!
You know...
You're such a prim and proper girl, being the class president and all that. Aren't you a little nervous, being all alone with me like this?
ごくっ
GULP
That's right...

This guy, Aoi Izumi, is the pampered son of a wealthy IT company CEO.
He's got more girlfriends than there are stars in the sky—and he's dumped even more girls than that! Well, according to the rumors, anyway.
They say he's a totally self-absorbed jerk!
If I'd known I was going to get stuck working at his summer home, I never would have agreed to this!
SCREAMING ON THE INSIDE
Hey.
I know we go to the same school, but we've never really had the chance to talk with each other. It's kind of a lucky coincidence that you wound up here, isn't it?
H-hey! What are you doing?!
W-wow... he's actually pretty good-looking close up like this...
We shouldn't waste this golden opportunity. Why don't we get to know each other a little better?

...he wants to make me another one of his "stars in the sky"?!
N-no...
STEP
W-what?!
Don't tell me... what he means is...
Why do you think?
GRIN
Just kidding!!
LET GO
Um...
BA-BUMP
Huh...?
PLOP
Don't worry. I have no intention of trying to make a move on you.
W... why not?

ZERO SEXIAH!
ゾッ
DONK
Nah. Doesn't exactly do it for me.
A girl like you who's got *zero sex appeal* whatsoever??
Wha...
Well! I'm soooooo sorry I'm not sexy enough for you!! I came here to work, so that's how I'm dressed—what's wrong with that?! Am I supposed to mop the floors in a miniskirt?! You can't exactly climb a mountain in high heels, ya know!!
ポイ
TOSS
ポイ
TOSS
ポイ
TOSS
ゴッ
POLISH
POLISH
ゴッ
PANT
ハー
PANT
ゼー
ピカ
SPARKLE
PANT
ハー
PANT
ゼー
ピカ
SPARKLE
WHAT IS *THAT* SUPPOSED TO MEAN?!?!?
ごあし
SCRUB
ごあし
SCRUB
ごあし
SCRUB

Wow! What gorgeous furniture!
It'll be a good experience for an average middle-class girl like Sakamoto Kōme (yours truly!) to rub shoulders with such a wealthy family.
SQUEAK
Maybe I'm even starting to look a little bit like a rich society girl myself...
Looks like you've got some free time on your hands.
Why don't you start some laundry and then get busy weeding the garden.
Y-Y-you...!
!!!
Huh?
Didn't anybody ever tell you that if you make weird faces in front of a mirror, it'll crack?
This mirror is an Italian antique worth 3,000,000 yen.
3,000,000 yen = US $30,000
Eep!!
WEIRD FACE
もんなの
!!
All right, all right! Jeez!!
...Thank goodness this mirror didn't crack.

SPACING OUT
Phew...
I can't believe I'm still taking this job seriously after all the things he's said to me. I must be out of my mind.
SKEEEE
SKEEEE
He's awful...
はた FLAP
はた FLAP
GLARE
That much money would buy X amount of sweet red bean buns at Kimura-ya...!
No problem.
I-I'm sorry.
And when he said that thing about the mirror that cost 3,000,000 yen, I couldn't even come up with a good comeback.
Maybe he's just one of those people who never let anybody get close to them.
Don't tell me you're done already??
What have I gotten myself into??
I'd heard he was mean, but I didn't realize he was *this* mean!!
Hey...
SOB
SOB

—No, that's fine for now. Go ahead and take a break.
Break?
FIGHTING STANCE
.....
Yes, sir! I'm all finished! Is there anything else I can do for you?
But how come he's here all by himself?
...this really is a beautiful house!
Now that I can stop and take another look around...
Phew...
CLINK
That was weird. All of a sudden he decided to be nice for some reason.

Izumi-kun! The phone's ringing!
RIIIIIIIING
GRAB
Yes! Hello?
Well, here goes nothing!
I don't know if I should be answering his phone, but...
SQUEAL
We're his groupies!
He could be hanging out with his groupies right now.
SQUEAL
RIIIING
Oh!
That's right, Ms. Girlfriend. Is Aoi there?
A-are you his father?
"Like father, like son"?? So this must be...
GRRR
I don't see him around right now, but I can take a message for him.
Oh, and by the way, I'm just here as a housekeeper. I wouldn't be caught dead going out with your son.
TOTAL BLUNTNESS
Wait, that's not him, that's a girl. Are you Aoi-kun's girlfriend?
A-Aoi-kun?!
So he brought you back to the house with him already? Well, like father, like son, I guess!
HEH
HEH
HEH
TWITCH

Well, he and I were supposed to spend some quality time together at the house, just the two of us, but something came up at work and I'm not going to be able to make it. I was going to tell him about it myself, but...
HA HA HA!
I like you! You've really got some spirit, girl!
...So did you want to leave a message or something?
I have to admit, he was a bit of a crybaby lone wolf-type when he was younger, though! HA HA HA!
Well, that's all right. I'm sure even Aoi-kun won't be too sad if he hears it from a delightful girl like you.
SMIRK
ニヤッ
I guess now I know why he's home alone.
And on top of that...
ガチャン
HANG UP
N-not much alike, are they?
Well.
CLICK
ガチャ
Well, thanks! I appreciate it!
BOOP
BOOP

Huh?
Where have you been hiding?
You just missed a very important phone call.
Why hello there, little lone wolf Aoi-kun. ♡
Don't tell me...
It was from your loving father. He did leave a message though... ♡
It went something along the lines of, "I won't be able to keep my promise to Aoi-kun. Oh, I do hope he won't be too sad and lonely without me."
SMIRK
Wow. I had no idea that the oh-so-cool Izumi-kun was actually a big fat CRYBABY LONER.
That was a long time ago!!
Jeez, Dad, what's wrong with you?!

Oh, you don't have to worry. Of course I wouldn't *dream* of mentioning this to anybody.
But it's too bad, really. You were supposed to be spending time here with your dad, and now you're stuck here with me instead.
But since I've already come all the way out here, and my work is all done...
...I think I'd like to stick around for a while and see what it's like to live the celebrity life. Get my drift?
Sakamoto... you...
EH HEH
I won't forget this.
Whoa! Scary!!
All right, all right. You can stay here as my guest.
But we've got to do something about that outfit.
Huh? But I don't really have anything else besides this...
SNAP
Don't worry. If it's stylists and beauticians you need...

First let's get you into a nice hot bath!
Eeeeeek!!
TOSS
TOSS
The jets in this bath refresh you with negative ion therapy.
Let me go ahead and take care of your nails while you're soaking.
...we've got a full staff right here.
What?!
We'll take good care of her, Izumi-sama!

Deep-tissue massages are good for both your skin and your hair.
And full-body spa treatments will improve your entire figure!
So how does it feel to be officially made over by a group of top-notch stylists?
SWISH
Now we'll give you the latest in nail art, hairstyling, and makeup.
Oh...

Wow!!
SMOOTH TALKERS
You already had a great foundation, so all we did was just polish you up a bit and bring out your natural beauty.
Really?
Wow! You look so cute!
I do?
Ladies, I think our work here is done! ♡
She's all ready, Izumi-kun!
Haha! Check *this* out, Izumi-kun!
Let's see if you still think I have zero sex appeal now!
カチャ
CREEEEAK...

Hmmm.
Yes, that's better. At least you look halfway decent now.
SHOCK
He really is a mean guy!!
CHOMP
Huh...?
You're right! She really looks amazing!
Aoi-san has such good taste. Now how about some accessories?
BA-BUMP
Seriously, though...
Don't you think you look a whole lot cuter than you did before?
FLUTTER
We'll go and straighten up.
Hey!
What am I getting all flustered about?

KISS
ちゅっ♡
This guy is a player, so of course he has a way with women. It's only natural that...
—Hmmm.
Why do you think?
Huh?!
He just *kissed* me!!
Why did you just do that?!
H-he...
LEAP
—!?
W-what are you doing?!

Not that same question again!
Why did he kiss me, anyway?
I... I don't know.
Well, isn't that what you're supposed to do when you like a girl?
Is he trying to say that he...
GRIN
What?!
I thought you were really...
Jeez, you really do take everything completely seriously, don't you?
SNICKER SNICKER
I just thought you looked cute, so I figured why not.
Don't be so naïve, Ms. Freshman Class President.

Um... excuse me, Sakamoto-sama...
CLATTER BANG
He's awful! I hate him! He's the worst boy I've ever met!!
CHOMP SMACK
CHEW
CHEW
SLAM
I oughtta kill him!!
SOB
And to think that was my first kiss, too!
BWAH
Speaking of Izumi, where the heck did he go, anyway?!
My $500-a-plate specially prepared meal...
Oh no...
EMPTY
Well, I'm not going to think about it anymore! I'll just think of it as a dog bite and forget it ever happened!!
BANG CRASH
That's right. I fully intend to enjoy my "celebrity lifestyle" summer and I'm more than happy to use him in order to do so!!
M-miss! That plate is supposed to be for Izumi-san!!

Well, I already ate your portion anyway, so that's probably a good thing.
But if you've been stuffing yourself on junk food, it's no wonder you're not hungry.
TOTAL MESS
It's OK. I'm not really hungry.
Why don't you go outside for a while or something?
What's the point in being away for the summer if you're just gonna spend all your time in here?
Look, I do this every year, so just shut up and leave me alone, OK?
If you come any closer, I'll kiss you again.
Eeek! Get away from me, you pervert!!
You really are a lone wolf, aren't you.
RRGH...

Saka –!
I'm not gonna leave you alone until you agree to come outside with me, Mr. Lone Wolf!
You guys can all just go home now, OK?
Come on, let's go!
It'd be a shame to let a place like this go unexplored!
This is great!
It's way too bright out here.

Look around you. You're surrounded by nature!
It's beautiful! It's astounding! Right?
Not really. I'd rather be inside watching the same thing on a big screen HD TV.
ANNOYED
You can't *smell* or *feel* nature through a television though, can you?!
SHOVE
What the—?!
SPLASH
ばっしゃーん!
A-ha-ha!
See? You just got to experience what water feels like!
You little...

Let's see how *you* like it!!
Eeeek!!
SPLASH
What are you doing?! You just ruined my new outfit!
Well, you deserved it.
BA-BUMP
...What's that all about?

Look!
He's supposed to be a mean guy.
So what does he think he's doing, smiling at me like that?
It's like he's trying to trick me or something.
The sun is setting.

Hun?
Well, you can thank me later for dragging you out here to see one.
...I didn't know the sunsets were so beautiful here.
Oh no!
My heel broke!
That's what you get for walking around in those shoes.
SNAP
And whose fault is it that I'm wearing these—
SWOOP
!?
!?
—Well, you can't walk on a broken heel, can you?
MOUTH HANGING OPEN

...Self-conscious...
W-what do I do?
BA-BUMP
I feel so...
I'll... I'll make you dinner!! Then we'll be even! OK?!
Huh?
But...
Look, it's not like you have to pay me back for carrying you or something, OK?
But...
So...
...if you're the one who volunteered to cook, then how did I wind up doing it all instead??

I'm sorry. I'm just a reeeeally really bad cook.
Then why did you say you were going to make me dinner in the first place??
Well, whatever. Let's eat!
EH HEH...
Wow, this looks great!
Well, I've been spending a lot of time by myself ever since I was little.
I used to watch the chefs and then imitate what they did. So I've done a lot of cooking.
Oh...
What a poor little kid you were. I feel so sorry for you.
Cut it out!
!!
This is delicious!!
CHOMP
...Really?
I mean it! You're a genius!!

Ooooh! I'm so happy!! ♡
You know, Sakamoto-san, you're a lot different outside of school.
HEH
Huh?
You're a strange one.
It's funny...
I feel like today I got to see a side of Izumi-kun that I never knew before.
Phew... I'm beat!
Do you want to go back to your room?
Not yet.
Come here.
GRAB
Huh?

H-hey!!
It's all your fault I'm so tired, so this is the least you can do.
Well, excuse me for wearing you out! You certainly *looked* like you were having a good time!
...Well, I was.
I thought he was a mean guy, but...
Thanks to you, Sakamoto-san...
...I haven't been lonely at all today.
...if that's true, then...

...Why does he make my heart pound like this?
Well, it's getting cold out here.
Let's go inside.
SIT UP
Wha...
What was that?!

I...
I-kinda thought he was gonna kiss me again...
So why didn't he??
BEEP
BEEP
SLAM
I missed you soooooo much!!
BA-BUMP
Aoi!
Huh?
Oh!
Well, I didn't hear from you before you left, so I looked up your address myself and came out for a surprise visit!
How did you...?
Oh.
Looks like the groupies have arrived.

You're not here on vacation with Aoi, are you?
N-no! Not at all!
Is that you, Sakamoto-san?
No way! What are you doing here?
Class President, Kome
I'm working here for the summer. It's just kind of a coincidence, that's all.
Oh, OK! That makes more sense.
No offense, but you guys don't really seem like a good match for each other, ya know?
FREEZE
SQUEEZE
W-who do you think you are? You might be rich kids, just like he is...
But Izumi-kun is just a regular guy at heart...
Hey, Aoi...
How about spending a little quality time together? Just you and me?

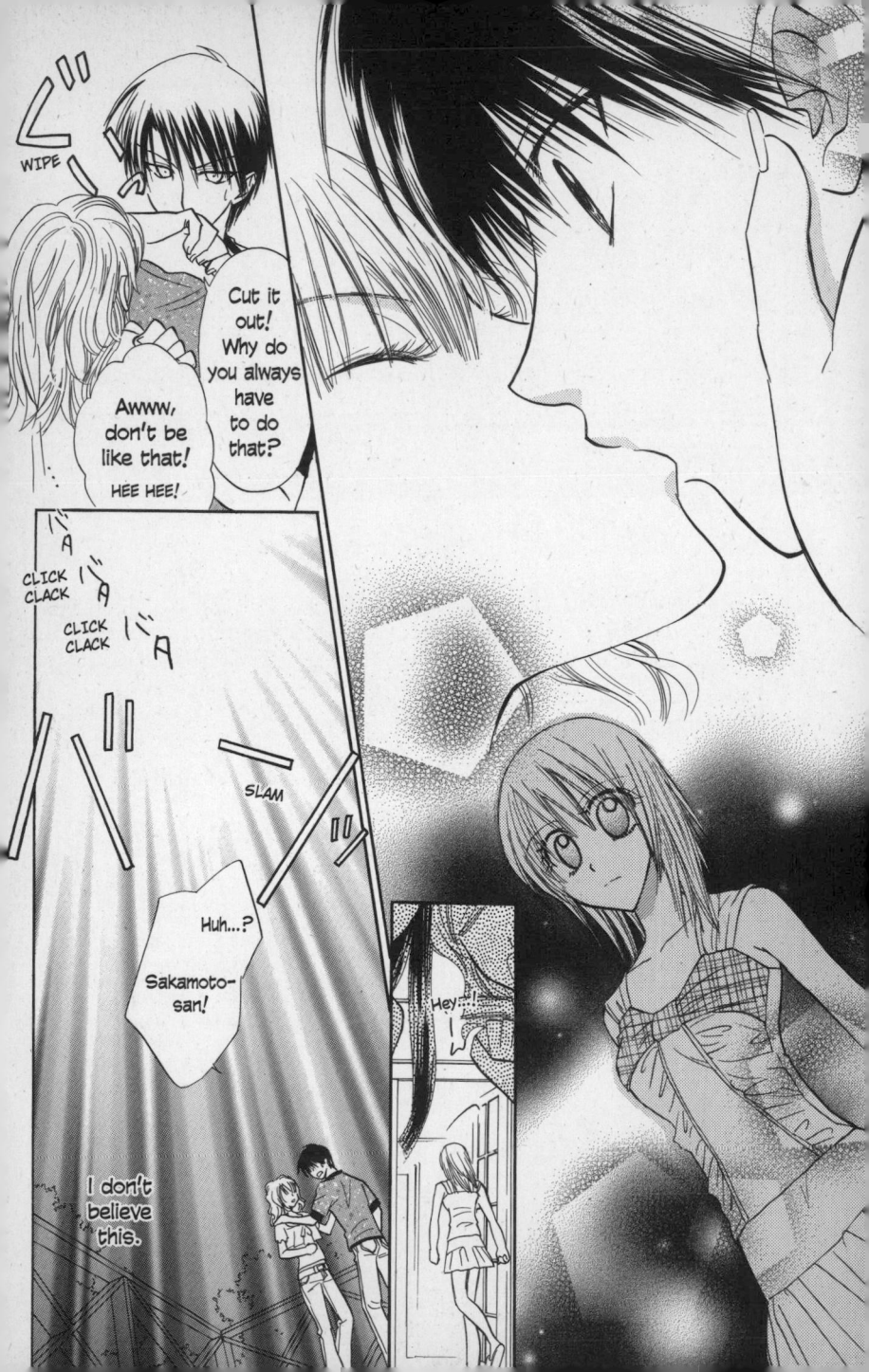
WIPE
Cut it out! Why do you always have to do that?
Awww, don't be like that!
HEE HEE!
CLICK CLACK
CLICK CLACK
SLAM
Huh...?
Sakamoto-san!
I don't believe this.
Hey...!

I really don't believe this! Aoi Izumi, you jerk!!
You...
you were kissing that girl.
Hey!
Sakamoto-san!!
GRAB
You idiot! Where do you think you're going? There's no bus or train running this late!
Huh?
Is that what you're upset about? That was more of a friendly greeting than anything.
I can't believe I actually wanted him to kiss me earlier.
Well, that's just not what a kiss means to me, OK?
Now I know what's going on here.

I would only kiss someone like that if I really, really liked them.
And I wouldn't want a guy I liked to kiss anybody else like that besides me.
Because I've already fallen for him.
—
And now it's too late to turn back.
I thought that just because I got to see a side of Izumi-kun that nobody else knows, that somehow that made me special.

OK, I kissed you.
Does that make you feel any better?

Well, now I've done it for sure.
BA-BUMP
M-my heart...
I can hear it beating...
BA-BUMP
I've kissed you twice, so now there's no going back.
...Wait a second.
What the heck does that mean?!
ぼっ
BLUSH
But maybe it's not just my heart that's beating so hard...
BA-BUMP

I want to see the look on his face.
Hey...
So why...
Let me see your face...
GRIN
Why do you think?
Why did you do that just now?

The guy I like can be mean sometimes.
You're...
You're so *mean*!!
But at the same time...
...he can also be pretty amazing.
★★ The End ★★

Glasses News ~ The Creation of "Four-Eyed Prince" ~

Glasses News Website: http://megane-ouji.cocolog-nifty.com/blog

To all my first-time readers as well as the long-time readers, I'd like to say a great big "Glasses"! (It's my special greeting!) This is Mizukami. As the end of 2006 was drawing near, a chance word from my Supervisor, S-san—

—caused this manga to be born. What's that you say? This is supposed to be a manga about glasses, but there weren't enough scenes with glasses in them? If you're one of the people who thinks so, then by all means, be sure to read the next volume! I promise to up the percentage of scenes featuring glasses by 200%.

~ Special Thanks ~

Ichiri Hashiba * Miki Fujimori
Naho Yamada * Hiromi Hiraiwa * Megumu Aya
&
Editor S & N * my family * my friends
&
You !!

Sachi's Glasses Observation Report

Today's Theme:
Just how bad is Akihiko's eyesight?

What do you want now?
Hey Sachi, what'd you do with my glasses?!
ANSWER!
0.002 in both eyes
Your eyesight is terrible!
Sempai... I'm over here...
As Akira he wears contacts, of course.
What?!
I couldn't. I just kinda felt my way through it.
How could you see anything during that costume contest??

Wataru Mizukami

Birthplace: Tokyo. Birthday: August 25. Debuted in 1995 with the Nakayoshi Manga Newcomer award-winning work *Never Give Up!* Best-known manga: *Let's Get Married!* Hobbies: tennis, driving, and shopping. Lately she's been planning to move to a new house.

Translation Notes

Japanese is a tricky language for most Westerners, and translation is often more art than science. For your edification and reading pleasure, here are notes on some of the places where we could have gone in a different direction, or where a Japanese cultural reference is used.

Sachi, page 7

"Sachi" is a nickname for the main character, Sachiko. The name "Sachiko" means "happy," so from that you can tell that Sachiko tends to have a bright and positive personality.

***Megane,* page 7, 169**

Megane is the Japanese word for "glasses." Since part of the reason for Sachiko's crush on her sempai is the fact that he wears glasses, it's safe to say that glasses (or *megane*) are a significant part of the story of *Four-Eyed Prince.*

Kabuki-chō Ichibangai, page 19

Kabuki-chō Ichibangai is the main street of the Kabuki-chō entertainment and red-light district in Tokyo. The neighborhood is called Kabuki-chō because at one point there was a plan to build a kabuki theater in that area, which was formerly known as Tsunohazu. The theater was never constructed, but the name Kabuki-chō stuck.

Master, page 20

In Japan, a bartender is generally referred to as "Master."

Trip to a hot spring, page 56

Taking a trip to a natural hot spring, or *onsen*, is a typical cultural activity in Japan. Friends, couples, or families travel to a town located near a hot spring and stay at an inn that has bathing facilities that are fed from the naturally heated spring waters. *Onsen* group bathing is a favorite way to relax and rejuvenate the body.

Kent Derricott, page 169

Kent Derricott, originally from Canada, gained fame as a television personality in Japan. He originally moved to Japan in 1983 to expand his import business, and subsequently became an actor and celebrity after a chance appearance on a Japanese variety show. Of course, he also wears glasses, just like the Four-Eyed Prince.

Preview of Volume 2

We're pleased to be able to present you a preview from Volume 2. Please check our website (www.delreymanga.com) to see when this volume will be available in English. For now you'll have to make do with Japanese.

さえない男に大変身☆

——あらアキラくんは？

キョロ キョロ

♪

さー帰りましょ彰彦先輩！

もー近所歩くのに毎回こんなのめんどくさいったら

そんなに必死になることかよ

だってせっかく…

そしてわたしは

この義理の兄に

片思い中…

べつにこれはデートじゃなくてただのお使いだろ？

ムキー!!

いいの！気分なの！

いってきまーす
しかし
毎度のことながら
みんなの反応の差が
フシギなんだよね
おい あぶないぞ！
え
パパ
水と神さま
だーって

メガネの先輩もこんなにステキじゃないですか!!
まったく世話のやける
うわっいまのしぐさ!!
なんて…なんて…

萌え――!!!
!?
いまの見ました!?
見た 見た!
メガネをおし上げるしぐさをあそこまでのレベルでこなすとは!
あなどれないわね～
ああの…?
びっくりしたわたしの心の声がもれたかと…
あっ われわれですか!?
イケメガネ萌え隊 隊長 田沼愛梨
イケメガネ萌え隊 隊員 小林川
イケメガネ萌え隊 隊員 森さやか
「イケメガネ…萌え隊」?
そうっ

イケてる！
メガネに!?
萌え 萌え♡
し隊！
な…なんじゃこいつら…
ぞろ
じんびき…
あ…いそぐので
待って——!!

SHUGO CHARA!

PEACH-PIT

Creators of *Dears* and *Rozen Maiden*

Everybody at Seiyo Elementary thinks that stylish and super-cool Amu has it all. But nobody knows the *real* Amu, a shy girl who wishes she had the courage to truly be herself. Changing Amu's life is going to take more than wishes and dreams—it's going to take a little magic! One morning, Amu finds a surprise in her bed: three strange little eggs. Each egg contains a Guardian Character, an angel-like being who can give her the power to be someone new. With the help of her Guardian Characters, Amu is about to discover that her true self is even more amazing than she ever dreamed.

Special extras in each volume! Read them all!

VISIT WWW.DELREYMANGA.COM TO:

- Read sample pages
- View release date calendars for upcoming volumes
- Sign up for Del Rey's free manga e-newsletter
- Find out the latest about new Del Rey Manga series

RATING T AGES 13+

DEL REY MANGA デルレイ

The Otaku's Choice

Shugo Chara! © 2006 PEACH-PIT/ KODANSHA LTD. All rights reserved.

Papillon

BY MIWA UEDA

BUTTERFLY, SPREAD YOUR WINGS!

Ageha is a shy tomboy, but her twin sister Hana is the ultimate ultra-glam teen queen. Hana loves being the center of attention so much that she'll do anything to keep Ageha in her shadow. But Ageha has a plan that will change her life forever and no one, not even Hana, can hold her back. . . .

• From the creator of *Peach Girl*

Special extras in each volume! Read them all!

VISIT WWW.DELREYMANGA.COM TO:
- Read sample pages
- View release date calendars for upcoming volumes
- Sign up for Del Rey's free manga e-newsletter
- Find out the latest about new Del Rey Manga series

RATING T AGES 13+

DEL REY DEL REY MANGA デルレイ

The Otaku's Choice™

Papillon © 2007 Miwa Ueda / KODANSHA LTD. All rights reserved.